JE
SNY

Snyder, Inez.
Grains to bread

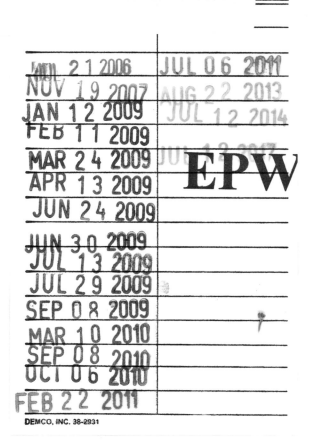

How Things Are Made

Grains to Bread

By Inez Snyder

Children's Press®
A Division of Scholastic Inc.
New York / Toronto / London / Auckland / Sydney
Mexico City / New Delhi / Hong Kong
Danbury, Connecticut

Photo Credits: Cover © Stock Food/Michael Carter; pp. 5, 9 © Stock Food/Beatriz Da Costa; p. 7 © Stock Food/Renee Cornet; p. 11 © David Noton/Getty Images; pp. 13, 15, 17 © Stock Food/Eising; p. 19 © image100 LTD; p. 21 © Robin Davies/Getty Images

Contributing Editor: Shira Laskin
Book Design: Christopher Logan

Library of Congress Cataloging-in-Publication Data

Snyder, Inez.
    Grains to bread / by Inez Snyder.
    p. cm. — (How things are made)
    Includes index.
    ISBN 0-516-25197-X (lib. bdg.) — ISBN 0-516-25527-4 (pbk.)
    1. Bread—Juvenile literature. 2. Grain—Juvenile literature. I. Title. II. Series.

    TX769.S76 2005
    641.8'15—dc22
                                                    2004010244

1 2 3 4 5 6 7 8 9 10 R 14 13 12 11 10 09 08 07 06 05

Contents

Bread is made from **grain**.

There are many kinds of grains.

Different grains can be used to make different types of bread.

Millet, **oats**, and **wheat** are grains.

Many people like bread made from wheat.

millet

wheat

oats

9

Wheat is grown in large fields.

Farmers use big machines to **harvest** the wheat.

A **mill** is used to make wheat grain into **flour**.

Flour is used to make bread.

13

First, the flour is mixed with water and **yeast**.

This makes bread **dough**.

Next, the dough
is **kneaded**.

After the dough is kneaded,
it must rise.

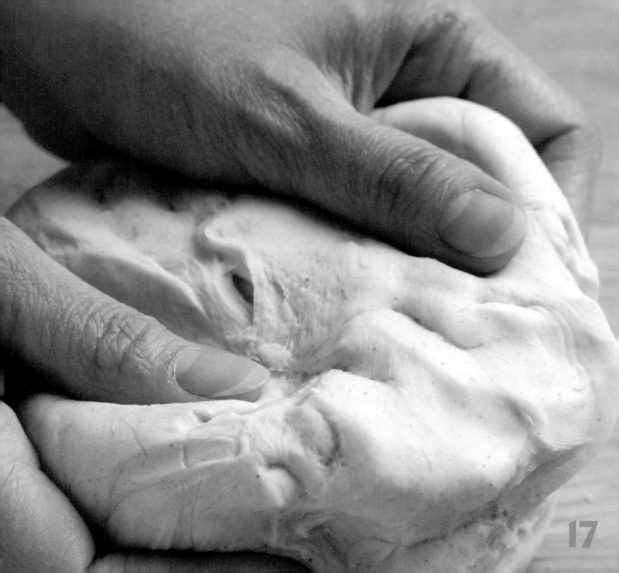

17

When the dough is finished rising, it is put into an oven to bake.

The finished bread is taken out of the oven.

The bread is done baking.

It is ready to eat.

Bread tastes good!

New Words

dough (**doh**) a thick, sticky mixture of flour, water, and other ingredients used to make bread

flour (**flou**-ur) a powder that you bake or cook with that is usually made from wheat

grain (**grayn**) a tiny seed of rice, corn, wheat, or other plants that is used for growing new plants or is eaten

harvest (**hahr**-vuhst) to pick or gather plants

kneaded (**need**-uhd) when dough is pressed, folded, and stretched until smooth

mill (**mil**) a machine used for grinding grain into flour

millet (**mil**-it) a grass like wheat, harvested for its grain, which is used for food

oats (**ohts**) grains of a kind of grass plant used as food

wheat (**weet**) a tall grass plant that is used to make flour, pasta, and some kinds of breakfast cereal

yeast (**yeest**) something used to make bread dough rise

To Find Out More

Books
Grains
by Robin Nelson
Lerner Publishing Group

The Wheat We Eat
by Allan Fowler
Children's Press

Web Site
Wheat Mania!: Kansas Association of Wheat Growers Educational Web Site
http://www.wheatmania.com
Learn about how wheat grows, how it is turned into flour, and more on this informative Web site.

Index

About the Author
Inez Snyder writes books to help children learn how to read.

Content Consultant
Jason Farrey, The Culinary Institute

Reading Consultants
Kris Flynn, Coordinator, Small School District Literacy, The San Diego County
Office of Education

Shelly Forys, Certified Reading Recovery Specialist, W.J. Zahnow Elementary
School, Waterloo, IL

Paulette Mansell, Certified Reading Recovery Specialist, and Early Literacy
Consultant, TX